D1535628

Delaney Street Press

Simplicity is Genius

*Nine Powerful Principles
for Clarifying Your Thoughts
and Simplifying Your Life*

By Criswell Freeman

DELANEY STREET PRESS
Nashville, TN 37211

ISBN: 1-58334-075-0

The ideas expressed in this book are not, in all cases, exact quotations, as some have been edited for clarity and brevity. In all cases, the author has attempted to maintain the speaker's original intent. In some cases, material for this book was obtained from secondary sources, primarily print media. While every effort was made to ensure the accuracy of these sources, the accuracy cannot be guaranteed. For additions, deletions, corrections or clarifications in future editions of this text, please write DELANEY STREET PRESS.

Cover Design by Bart Dawson
Layout and Typesetting by Sue Gerdes

Printed in the United States of America
1 2 3 4 5 6 7 8 9 10 • 00 01 02 03 04

ACKNOWLEDGMENTS

The author gratefully acknowledges the helpful support of Angela Beasley Freeman, Dick and Mary Freeman, Mary Susan Freeman, Carli Freeman, Jim Gallery, and the entire team of professionals at DELANEY STREET PRESS and WALNUT GROVE PRESS.

Dedicated to the Memory of
Don Pippin

Table of Contents

Make everything
as simple as possible,
but not simpler.

Albert Einstein

Your Complicated World

You live in a world where simplicity is in short supply. Think for a moment about the complexity of your everyday life and compare it to the lives of ancestors who lived only a hundred short years ago. Certainly, you are the beneficiary of many technological innovations, but those innovations have a price: in all likelihood, your world is highly complex. Consider the following:

1. From the moment you wake up in the morning until the time you lay your head on the pillow at night, you are the target of an endless stream of advertising information. Each message is intended to grab your attention in order to convince you to purchase things you didn't know you needed (and probably don't).

2. Unless you happen to be a hermit living on a deserted island, you are a tax-paying citizen of a well-meaning but profoundly complicated government with excruciatingly complex tax and legal codes. A hundred years ago, income taxes, for all practical purposes, didn't exist; today, whether you realize it or not, you are a part-time bookkeeper for the government.

3. The pace of technology is ever-quickening, perhaps leaving you with the uneasy feeling that the more you learn about high-tech matters, the more you need to learn.

4. You have at your fingertips a broad range of communication tools that can both improve your life and monopolize your time. Communication with your fellow human beings has never been cheaper or easier. Like it or not, you are a part of a global communication network with literally hundreds of thousands of potential callers vying for your attention.

5. You are more likely than your forefathers to be touched — directly or indirectly —by someone's divorce. Non-traditional family structures create a variety of complications not common to earlier generations.

6. Essential aspects of your life, including personal matters such as health care, are subject to an ever-increasing flood of rules and regulations from both the public and private sectors.

7. To complicate matters further, you — as a member of a prosperous generation — may have a greater ability than your forefathers to spend money on purchases that you do not

really need. More spending means more items cluttering the landscape of your life.

Unless you take firm control of your time and your life, you may be overwhelmed by a tidal wave of complexity that threatens your happiness. The ideas on the following pages are intended to help you sort through the clutter, separate important matters from unimportant ones, and, in doing so, invest your time and effort on the things that are important to you and your loved ones.

Because you have picked up this little book, you probably feel a need to simplify some aspect of your life. If so, congratulations. Simplicity is genius. By simplifying your life, you are destined to improve it.

Nine Powerful Principles
for Clarifying Your Thoughts
and Simplifying Your Life

Principle 1

Unclutter Your Mind

A cluttered life is the physical manifestation of a cluttered mind. Therefore, the first task in simplifying your life is to clarify your thoughts.

If your thoughts are disorganized, you will find difficulty in distinguishing imagined problems from real ones, big troubles from small ones, important tasks from trivial ones. You'll soon find yourself caught up in an unproductive, unhappy maelstrom of wasted motion. The antidote to this frustration is simple: clearheaded, rational thinking.

Rational thought is elusive in the hustle and bustle of a fast-paced world. Clear thinking evades the person who is tired, stressed, or both. Without the benefit of rational thought, a person tends to make imprudent decisions and act upon those decisions in haste — with predictably disappointing results.

A rested, quiet mind, on the other hand, is a powerful remedy to the everyday stresses that might otherwise interfere with sound decision-making. Thankfully, clear thinking is available to almost anyone who regularly takes a few minutes each morning to organize his or her thoughts. The early morning is the perfect time to inspire, educate, and organize oneself.

If you find yourself in extremely stressful circumstances, a regular time of contemplation and study may not be enough; you may wish to consult a trusted friend, a clergyman, or an impartial professional counselor. But for the everyday stresses of life, you'll find that a daily dose of early-morning meditation will allow you to organize your time, clarify your objectives, and motivate yourself to act upon your most important priorities.

Clear perspective is a powerful tool for improving and ultimately simplifying your life. The following quotations are reminders of the great benefits you reap when you learn regularly, think rationally, and behave accordingly.

Life is a festival
only to the wise.
Ralph Waldo Emerson

What we see depends mainly upon
what we look for.

John Lubbock

We don't see things as they are,
we see things as we are.

Anaïs Nin

Knowledge comes by eyes always open
and working hands, and there is
no knowledge that is not power.

Jeremy Taylor

Time given to thought is the greatest
time saver of all.

Norman Cousins

The price of wisdom is eternal thought.

Frank Birch

Wisdom is acquired by meditation.

Publilius Syrus

I do not think much of a man who
is not wiser today than
he was yesterday.
Abraham Lincoln

As long as you live, keep learning
how to live.
Seneca

Always keep learning.
It keeps you young.
Patty Berg

A man's wisdom is his best friend;
folly his worst enemy.
William J. Temple

A man, though wise, should never
be ashamed of learning more.
Sophocles

Happy is the man that gains wisdom
and the man that gets understanding.
Proverbs 3:13

Learning is either
a continual thing
or it is nothing.

Frank Tyger

Wisdom is the supreme
part of happiness.
Sophocles

Tips for Uncluttering Your Mind

1. Begin each day with a few minutes of quiet time to organize your thoughts. During this time, read at least one uplifting passage and thus begin your day on a positive, productive note.
2. During your quiet time, keep a brief written journal of your thoughts and actions. Catch yourself whenever you tend to exaggerate your problems or lose sight of the big picture.
3. Assiduously divide your areas of concern into two categories: those you can control and those you cannot. Resolve never to waste time or energy worrying about the latter.
4. Get adequate rest. Without it, you'll tend to become easily frustrated, anxious, and irritable. Sleep deprivation makes clear thinking difficult; too much sleep deprivation makes clear thinking impossible.

Principle 2

Clarify Your Personal Mission

It has been said, "If you don't know where you want to go, any road will take you there." Do you know exactly where you intend to go in life, and would you recognize your destination if you arrived there? If not, it's time to draft a clearly-written personal mission statement. This statement should contain a brief overview of your attitudes toward the most important areas of your life, including spiritual, family, professional, health-related, financial, and social concerns.

For thousands of years, the writers of wisdom literature have reminded us that each person's life is a unique journey — your life is no different. Your journey from cradle to grave can and should be a grand and satisfying adventure. But grand adventures don't happen by accident. If you seek to leave your mark upon the world, you'll need to decide exactly what kind of mark you intend to make.

In the process of formulating your personal mission statement, you will define those things which should assume utmost importance in your life. Once your mission statement is completed, you may choose to go further by drafting a clearly defined set of personal goals. Meaningful goals of short, medium, and long-term duration serve as a road map through life, thus ensuring that the road you take will be one of your own choosing.

The most powerful goals are those which are written, measurable, achievable, but challenging. Once you've completed your written mission statement and goals, review them often. You'll be reminded of the things that really matter in your life. And you'll ensure that *your* journey is worthy of its traveler.

Make your life a mission — not an intermission.

Arnold Glasgow

Great minds
have purposes;
others have wishes.
Washington Irving

What we are is God's gift to us.
What we become is our gift to God.
Eleanor Powell

Nobody's gonna live for you.
Dolly Parton

Live out your life in its full meaning.
It is God's life.
Josiah Royce

If you're not in the parade,
   you watch the parade. That's life.
                                    Mike Ditka

Only I can change my life.
      No one can do it for me.
                              Carol Burnett

Plunge boldly into the thick of life!
                                  Goethe

He who keeps his eye fixed on the
far horizon will find his right road.
Dag Hammarskjold

I'll walk where my own nature would
be leading; it vexes me to choose
another guide.
Emily Brontë

Be what you are. This is the first step
in being better than you are.
Julius Charles Hare

The greatest thing in the world is to know how to be oneself.

Michel de Montaigne

Fear not that thy life
shall come to an end,
but rather fear that
it shall never have
a beginning.

Cardinal Newman

This is the true joy in life: being used for a purpose recognized by yourself as a mighty one.

George Bernard Shaw

Purpose begins with
clarity. Clarity means
having a specific image
of what we want.
Most of us don't
have that.

Richard J. Leider

Do not act as if you had
    a thousand years to live.
                    Marcus Aurelius

The purpose of life is a life of purpose.
                    Robert Byrne

The great and glorious masterpiece
of man is how to live with a purpose.
                    Michel de Montaigne

May you live
all the days
of your life.

Jonathan Swift

Tips for Goal-Setting and for a Personal Mission Statement

1. Try to make your personal mission statement a powerful, concise document. Continually refine it until it accurately reflects your lifetime mission in as few words as possible.
2. Read your mission statement regularly and commit it to memory.
3. Use the mission statement as a basis for long, medium, and short-term goals. Put these goals on paper. Review them often.
4. Where possible, make your goals specific, measurable, and challenging — but also make them attainable.
5. Short-term goals should help you accomplish medium-term goals; medium-term goals should help you accomplish long-term goals; long-term goals should be congruent with your personal mission statement.

Principle 3

Prioritize or Be Prioritized

On your daily to-do list, all items are not created equal: Certain tasks are extremely important while others are not. Therefore, it's imperative that you prioritize your daily activities and complete each task in the approximate order of its importance.

The principle of doing first things first is simple in theory but more complicated in practice. Well-meaning family, friends, and coworkers have a way of making unexpected demands upon your time. Furthermore, each day has it own share of minor emergencies; these urgent matters tend to draw your attention away from more important ones. On paper, prioritizing is simple, but in the real world, acting upon those priorities requires maturity, patience, and determination.

If you fail to prioritize your day, life will automatically do the job for you. So your choice is simple: Prioritize or be prioritized. It's a choice that will help determine the quality of your life.

How can you move closer to your lifetime goals? Each day provides a fresh opportunity.

Alan Lakein

Putting first things first
is an issue at the very
heart of life.

Stephen Covey

Trim away the useless branches and throw your whole force of power into something that counts.

Walter J. Johnson

A man should remove not only
unnecessary acts, but also unnecessary
thoughts, so that superfluous activity
will not follow.
Marcus Aurelius

The real essence of work
is concentrated energy.
Walter Begehot

Become so wrapped up in something
that you forget to be afraid.
Lady Bird Johnson

Control over your life starts
      with planning.

Alan Lakein

We are not creatures of circumstance;
we are creators of circumstance.

Benjamin Disraeli

One today is worth two tomorrows.
Ben Franklin

Time is so precious that God deals it out
only second by second.
Bishop Fulton J. Sheen

A wise person does at once what a fool
does at last. Both do the same thing,
only at different times.
John Dalberg Acton

There's time enough,
but none to spare.

Charles W. Chesnutt

Great artists treasure their time
with a bitter and snarling miserliness.
Catherine Drinker Bowen

A schedule defends from chaos and
whim. It is a net for catching days.
It is a scaffolding on which a worker
can stand and labor with both hands
at sections of time.
Annie Dillard

There is no royal road to anything.
One thing at a time, and all things
in succession. That which
grows slowly endures.
J. G. Holland

When you learn to use your time
more carefully, time seems to expand.
Richard J. Leider

I must govern the clock,
not be governed by it.
Golda Meir

To know what you prefer, instead of
humbly saying "Amen" to what the world
tells you that you ought to prefer,
is to keep your soul alive.
Robert Louis Stevenson

Ask yourself this question: "What is the best use of my time right now?"

Alan Lakein

Tips for Prioritizing Your Life

1. Use your personal mission statement as a guide for defining high-priority activities that will move you toward your short, medium, and long-term goals.
2. Begin each work day with a simple to-do list. This list should help guide you toward the ultimate completion of your short, medium, and long-term goals — one day at a time. Rank the items on the list in order of priority and proceed accordingly.
3. When unexpected interruptions occur, as they will, don't become frustrated. Simply tend to the interruptions as quickly as possible and then get back to work on high-priority tasks.
4. Avoid the temptation to engage in time-wasting low-priority activities during working hours. Although low-priority work is often easier or less risky, it ultimately bears bitter fruit.
5. If possible, establish a certain time each day when you remove yourself from all distractions; during this time, concentrate exclusively on high-priority activities.

⤞⤝

Principle 4

Learn to Say "No"

The greatest single timesaving tool — and perhaps the most underutilized — is the word "No." Until you learn to say "No" politely yet firmly, you will find yourself bogged down with a seemingly endless string of commitments that fill your calendar and rule your life.

Individuals who overcommit themselves lead lives filled with endless complications: They are chronically overworked, under-appreciated, over-stressed, and underpaid.

So why not simplify your life by making a simple yet powerful pledge: Promise to reclaim your days by learning to say "No" to those things that you lack the time or the desire to do well. Treat your time as you would treat any other price-less asset and then watch the changes that a simple two-letter word can make in your life.

Besides the noble art of getting things done, there is the noble art of leaving certain things undone.

Lin Yü-t'ang

Everyone has a right
to his own course
of action.

Molière

You have a right to judge whether you are responsible for finding solutions to other people's problems.

Manuel J. Smith

It's important not to let other people fritter away your time, but when you say "No," you have to make it stick without seeming ruthless.
Alan Lakein

Nothing becomes an obligation simply because someone tells you it is.
David Seabury

All is disgust when one leaves his own nature and does things that misfit it.
Seneca

Never assume a
responsibility you can't
see through, and when
you refuse, be firm.

David Seabury

You have a right to say "No" without feeling guilty.

Manuel J. Smith

Tips for Learning to Say "No"

1. Never undertake a major obligation of any kind without first taking sufficient time to carefully consider whether or not you should commit to it. The bigger the obligation, the more days you should take to decide. If someone presses you for an answer before you are ready, your automatic response should be "No."

2. If you are burdened with a "people-pleasing" personality, outgrow it. Realize that you can't please all of the people all of the time, nor should you attempt to do so.

3. Remember that it is more important to be respected than to be liked.

4. Remember that you have a right to say "No" to requests that you consider unreasonable or inconvenient. Don't feel guilty for asserting that right, and don't feel compelled to fabricate excuses for your decisions.

Principle 5

Cut the Clutter

If there is a secret to effective work, that secret is organization. Too much clutter makes effective work impossible. The greater the amount of disorder in your life, the greater will be the difficulties in accomplishing your goals. But when you introduce organization into your daily affairs, you will begin reaping surprising dividends.

No one can organize your life but you. It's up to you, and nobody else, to invest the time and energy required to arrange your workplace and your home place in an orderly fashion. So clean out that closet. Clear off that desk. Handle a piece of paper one time and be done with it. Keep an accurate daily calendar and stick by your appointments. In short, spend more than a little time each day organizing yourself: It's well worth the effort.

Disorganization invites frustration. So if you're looking for a surefire way to clean up your life, clean out the clutter. Organization is good for the soul.

Good people order and arrange.

Confucius

Simplicity is the ultimate sophistication.

Leonardo da Vinci

Order means light and peace, inward liberty and free command over one's self; order is power.

Henri Frédéric Amiel

Order and simplification
are the first steps
toward the mastery
of a subject.

Thomas Mann

Good order is the foundation
of all good things.
Edmund Burke

Order is the sanity of the mind, the
health of the body, the peace of the city,
the security of the state.
Southey

A great man is an organized man.
Bulwer

The organized human being doesn't waste his energy, but is forever improving himself.

George Mathew Adams

Method is like packing things in a box;
a good packer will get in half again
as much as a bad one.

William Cecil

Almost all men are intelligent.
It is method that they lack.

F. W. Nichol

Method will teach you to win time.

Goethe

I am working to
improve my methods,
and every hour I save is
an hour added to
my life.

Ayn Rand

Order is heaven's
first law.

Alexander Pope

How happy we
can make our lives,
and the lives of those
around us, merely by
self-organization.

George Mathew Adams

Tips for Cutting the Clutter

1. If your home or office is filled with clutter, take an entire day and dedicate it to an initial cleanup operation. This commitment to clutter-free living will get you started on the right foot.
2. Learn to handle each piece of paper only once. The habit of leaving stacks of unfinished paperwork in piles upon your desk has an unintended consequence: It turns your work space into little more than a rectangular-shaped, horizontal waste bin. And as papers lie about unattended, you are sapped of valuable time and precious psychological energy.
3. Designate a place for those items that you use most often; make it a habit to return those items to their proper place after every use.
4. Be quick to give away things you no longer use. Someone needs those items more than you do, and besides, a good "spring cleaning" is therapeutic.

☙❧

Principle 6

Do It Now (And Get on With Life)

The habit of procrastination takes a two-fold toll on its victims. First, important work goes unfinished; second (and more importantly), valuable energy is wasted in the process of putting-off the things that remain undone.

Procrastination results from an individual's short-sighted attempt to postpone temporary discomfort. What results is a senseless cycle of delay and worry. A more logical approach, of course, is to attack the most unpleasant tasks of life first, thus freeing the mind for more appealing activities later.

Procrastination is, at its core, a struggle against oneself — the only antidote is action. Once you acquire the habit of doing what needs to be done when it needs to be done, you will avoid untold trouble, worry, and stress. So learn to defeat procrastination by paying less attention to your fears and more attention to your responsibilities. Life punishes procrastinators just as surely as it rewards men and women of action — and it does so sooner rather than later.

Nothing is so fatiguing
as the hanging on of an
uncompleted task.

William James

Whatever you can do,
or dream you can, begin
it. Boldness has genius,
power, and magic in it.

Goethe

Fortune sides with him who dares.
Virgil

Act decidedly and take the
consequences. No good deed was
ever done by hesitation.
Thomas Henry Huxley

To know what needs to be done, and
then to do it, comprises the
whole philosophy
of a practical life.
William Osler

Procrastination is opportunity's assassin.
Victor Kiam

The important thing is somehow
to begin.
Henry Moore

As long as you start, you are all right.
The juice will come.
Ernest Hemingway

Knowing is not enough; we must apply.
Willing is not enough; we must do.

Goethe

Do noble things, do not dream them
all day long.

Charles Kingsley

Action is eloquence.

William Shakespeare

An acre of
performance is worth
a whole world of
promise.

W. D. Howells

You may delay, but time will not.
Ben Franklin

Once a decision is reached,
stop worrying and start working.
William James

Try not to do too many things at once.
Know what you want: the number one
thing today and tomorrow.
Persevere and get it done.
George Allen

Rhetoric is a poor substitute
for action.
Teddy Roosevelt

If you want to do something, do it!
Plato

The wise man does immediately
what the fool does eventually.
Baltasar Gracián

The man who will not execute his
resolutions when they are fresh upon
him can have no hope of
doing them afterwards.
Marie Edgeworth

Words gain credibility by deed.
Terrence

Begin to weave and God will give the thread.

German Proverb

When I am idle and shiftless,
my affairs become confused. When
I work, I get results...not great results,
but enough to encourage me.
Edgar Watson Howe

He who desires but acts not
breeds pestilence.
William Blake

Can anything be sadder than work
unfinished? Yes; work never begun.
Christina Rosetti

Today is when everything that's going to happen from now on begins.

Harvey Firestone, Jr.

Tips for Getting Things Done

1. When faced with distasteful tasks, do them immediately. Otherwise, you'll be tempted to procrastinate, thus ruining your day and wasting untold amounts of energy in the process of fighting against yourself.

2. Avoid the trap of perfectionism. Be willing to do your best, and be satisfied with the results.

3. If you don't already own one, purchase the best daily or weekly planning system you can find. If used properly, a planning calendar is worth many times what you pay for it.

4. Start each work day with a clearly written "to-do" list, ranked according to importance. At lunch time, take a moment to collect your thoughts, reexamine your list, and refocus your efforts on the most important things you wish to accomplish during the remainder of the day.

Principle 7

Control Your Possessions Before They Control You

Thomas Carlyle noted, "Man is a tool-using animal; without tools he is nothing, with tools he is all." Carlyle understood that mankind depends upon a wide assortment of material goods to provide ease, comfort, security, and entertainment. Our material possessions improve our lives in countless ways, but when those possessions begin to assert undo control over our daily affairs, it's time to declare, "Enough stuff!"

Whenever a person becomes absorbed with the acquisition of things, complications arise. Each new acquisition costs money or time, often both. To further complicate matters, many items can be purchased, not with real money, but with something much more insidious: debt. Debt — especially consumer debt used to purchase depreciating assets — is a modern-day form of indentured servitude.

If you're looking for a surefire, time-tested way to simplify your life and thereby improve your world, learn to control your possessions before they control you. Purchase only those things that make a significant contribution to your well-being and the well-being of your family. Never spend more than you make. Understand the folly in buying consumer goods on credit. And never use credit cards as a way of financing your lifestyle.

Ask yourself this simple question: "Do I own my possessions, or do they own me?" If you don't like the answer you receive, make an ironclad promise to stop acquiring and start divesting. As you simplify your life, you'll be amazed at the things you can do without. You'll be pleasantly surprised at the sense of satisfaction that accompanies your new-found moderation. And you'll understand firsthand that when it comes to material possessions, paradox becomes reality: More often than not, less is more than more, and no less frequently, more is less than less.

Things are in the saddle
and ride mankind.
Ralph Waldo Emerson

The cost of a thing
is the amount of life
that must be exchanged
for it.

Henry David Thoreau

I am nearest to the gods in that I have the fewest wants.

Socrates

I believe that a simple and unassuming
manner of life is best for everyone,
best both for the body and the mind.
Albert Einstein

Reduce the complexity of life
by eliminating the needless
wants of life, and the labors of life
reduce themselves.
Edwin Way Teale

Our lives are frittered
away by detail....
Simplify, simplify,
simplify...simplicity
of life and evolution
of purpose.

Henry David Thoreau

The wisdom of life
consists in
the elimination
of nonessentials.

Lin Yü-t'ang

There is no greatness where there is
no simplicity.

Leo Tolstoy

Simplicity, carried to its extreme,
becomes elegance.

Jon Franklin

Simplicity is the peak of civilization.

Jessie Stampter

Happily for our blessedness,
  the joy of possession soon fades.
                              George Macdonald

The possessions of mortals
          are mortal.
                              Metrodorus

Let the moment come
when nothing is left but
life, and you will not
worry over the fate of
material possessions.

Eddie Rickenbacher

The wise man carries his possessions within him.

Bias of Priene

It is not the man
who has little, but he
who desires more,
who is poor.

Seneca

Tips for Controlling Your Possessions (Before They Control You)

1. Never borrow money to buy items that go down in value (this includes such things as new cars, boats, or clothes). If you find yourself in need of such an item but cannot afford to pay cash for it, find a less expensive alternative or do without.
2. Before making any purchase, consider not only the initial cost, but also the cost of upkeep and the amount of time required to do so.
3. Earn more than you spend. To do otherwise is to invite financial chaos into your life.
4. Conduct regular and vigorous "spring cleanings." Consider such activities normal events, not reserved for springtime.

Principle 8

Uncomplicate Your Relationships

Some of life's greatest complications result not from physical clutter, but from the chaos created by a small number of disorganized people who bring havoc in their own lives and, in turn, transfer that chaos to others. "Chaos-creators" are usually well-meaning friends, coworkers, or relatives who, for a variety of reasons, find themselves overwhelmed by the demands of life. Their lives seem always to be in turmoil, and, if we're not careful, their problems will soon become our problems, too.

The fact that a few of your associates are unable to manage their own affairs in a mature, common-sense fashion does not necessarily mean that you are required to save them from themselves. Of course, you may choose to lend a helping hand to whomever you wish; to do so is sometimes admirable. But you need not feel guilty for distancing yourself from people who repeatedly bring havoc into your life. It is your inalienable right to live free of personal chaos that is not of your own making.

People who feel overwhelmed by life almost always seek out saviors to rescue them from the responsibilities of everyday living. Unfortunately, what begins as a single rescue attempt may evolve into a series of unsuccessful salvage operations. In extreme cases, when individuals are incapable of caring for their own physical needs, we, as members of a caring society, are obliged to help. But when mentally competent adults are unwilling to modify their behaviors in order to meet the challenges of everyday life, we cannot force them to change.

Chaos is contagious: Your neighbor's chaotic lifestyle will become yours if you let it. So if you find yourself living in a world cluttered with the emotional litter of others, distance yourself from the chaos before it pulls you under. Whenever you find yourself dealing with difficult people, be strong, take a stand, set boundaries, and never feel guilty for doing so. Otherwise, you will forever find yourself trying to solve other people's problems while creating untold problems of your own.

Misery is a communicable disease.

Martha Graham

The meeting of two personalities is like the contact of two chemicals: If there is any reaction, both are transformed.

Carl Jung

A difficult person's troublesome behavior is habitual and affects most of the people around them.

Robert M. Bramson

We have no more right to consume
happiness without producing it than
we do to consume wealth
without producing it.
George Bernard Shaw

No human being can *make*
another one happy.
W. H. Auden

Some people simply have a highly
developed instinct for being unhappy.
Saki

It is better to offer no excuse
                than a bad one.
                              George Washington

The first requisite of a good citizen is
that he be willing to pull his own weight.
                              Teddy Roosevelt

Responsibility is the price of freedom.
Elbert Hubbard

Life is the sum of one's choices.
Albert Camus

Pardon one offense and you encourage
the commission of many.
Publilius Syrus

Tips for Uncomplicating Your Relationships

1. Don't feel guilty if you choose not to become involved in another person's chaos. If someone seeks to enlist you as a "savior" when you would prefer not to be cast in that light, it is your perfect right to say "No."
2. On the job, identify those individuals who habitually bring their personal chaos into the workplace. Realize that since you cannot change the behavior of your coworkers, your best alternative is to avoid being drawn into their personal turmoil.
3. If you supervise a person who brings chaos to the workplace, develop a clear understanding of what is acceptable conduct and what is not.
4. Remember that excuse-making is often a subtle form of dishonesty. Make clear to those around you that dishonesty on any level will not be glossed over or tolerated.
5. If close relatives make a habit of bringing chaos into your life, develop a clear understanding

of the behaviors you're willing to accept and those you're unwilling to accept. Communicate your decision and stand your ground, even if it means threatening the relationship.

6. Never accept blatant dishonesty as a part of any relationship, and never accept physical or emotional abuse from anyone, especially close relatives.

Principle 9

Control Your Appetites Before They Control You

Moderation is the royal road to the enlightened life: Temperance is wisdom in action. Intemperance, on the other hand, can be a deadly, senseless game.

Taken to the extreme, immoderate consumption evolves into addiction. And addiction quickly becomes the single all-consuming complication in the life of the addicted person.

Too many individuals have been victimized by their inability to say "No" to alcohol, drugs, gambling, or other assorted bad habits. Whatever forms they take, addictions always have tragic implications.

If you sincerely seek the joys that a simple life can yield, you must learn to control your appetites before they control you. Good habits, like bad ones, are self-perpetuating. The sooner you acquire the habit of moderation, the better your chances for a long and happy life.

The chains of habit
are too weak to be felt
until they are
too strong
to be broken.

Johnson

Habit is a cable; we weave a thread of it each day, and at last we cannot break it.
Thomas Mann

Habits change into character.
Ovid

Habit is either the best of servants
or the worst of masters.
Nathaniel Emmons

Moderation is the key
to lasting enjoyment.

Hosea Ballou

Happiness:
a way station between
too little and
too much.

Channing Pollack

If sweetness is excessive,
it is no longer sweetness.
African Proverb

Too little and too much
spoil everything.
Danish Proverb

Use, do not abuse....

Voltaire

Enough is as good
as a feast.

John Heywood

Tips for Controlling Your Appetites

1. If a trusted friend or relative suggests that you have a problem with the consumption of food, alcohol, or drugs, or that you have a problem with gambling, seek a second opinion from a trained professional.
2. If a trained mental health professional suggests that you may have a problem with addictive behavior, seek treatment immediately.
3. If you use tobacco products, take whatever measures are necessary to stop. Smoking is an expensive exercise in self-inflicted poor health.
4. Remember that ultimately you and you alone are responsible for controlling your appetites. Others may warn you, help you, or encourage you, but in the end, the habits that rule your life are the very same habits that you yourself have formed. Since you formed these habits, you can also break them — if you decide to do so.

Sources

About the Author

Criswell Freeman is a Doctor of Clinical Psychology living in Nashville, Tennessee. In addition to this text, Dr. Freeman is also the author of many other titles including his bestselling self help book *When Life Throws You a Curveball, Hit It.*

About
DELANEY STREET PRESS

DELANEY STREET PRESS publishes books designed to inspire and entertain readers of all ages. DELANEY STREET books are distributed by WALNUT GROVE PRESS. For more information, call 1-800-256-8584.